EDGE BOOKS™

UNSOLVED CRIME MYSTERIES

by Sean Stewart Price

Consultant:
Tim Solie
Adjunct Professor of History
Minnesota State University, Mankato

CAPSTONE PRESS
a capstone imprint

Edge Books are published by Capstone Press,
1710 Roe Crest Drive, North Mankato, Minnesota 56003
www.capstonepub.com

Library of Congress Cataloging-in-Publication Data
Price, Sean.
   Unsolved crime mysteries / by Sean Stewart Price.
      pages cm.—(Edge books. Unsolved mystery files)
   Includes bibliographical references and index.
   Summary: "Describes mysterious criminals and unsolved crimes from around the world"—Provided by
publisher.
   ISBN 978-1-4914-4263-0 (library binding)
   ISBN 978-1-4914-4339-2 (paperback)
   ISBN 978-1-4914-4319-4 (eBook PDF)
1. Crime—Juvenile literature. 2. Robbery—Juvenile literature. I. Title
   HV6251.P75 2016
   364.1—dc23   2014048933

Editorial Credits
Alesha Sullivan, editor; Sarah Bennett, designer; Gina Kammer,
media researcher; Morgan Walters, production specialist

Photo Credits
Alamy: Rex/© Daily Mail, 18; AP Photo: Paul Faith, 11; Corbis: © Bettmann, cover, 9; Getty Images:
Boston Globe, 17; Newscom: ZUMA Press/Kevin Horan, 22; Shutterstock: Claire McAdams, (fog
smoky background) throughout, Derek L Miller, 14, Designsstock, 23, detchana wangkheeree, 15, igor.
stevanovic, (background) 4-5, Imfoto, 28, Kunertus, 13, kuzmichs, (background) 14-15, 16-17, lapas77, 21,
Lester Balajadia, 25, Mark Heider, (Earth map) throughout, MisterElements, (ink splatters) throughout,
Peter Kim, (background) 18-19, 20-21, Ricardo Reitmeyer, 6, Roobcio, (grunge background) throughout,
Sashkin, (vault) 12-13, Serjio74, cover, Toniflap, 27, 29, tusharkoley, 8-9, Ursa Major, (worn background)
throughout; Springfield PD, 25

Contents

Criminal Behavior

Some criminals are really easy to catch. One bank robber in Nebraska bragged about her crime on YouTube. Police tracked her down pretty quickly thanks to the photos she provided. Then there were four bank robbers in Houston, Texas, who got caught after posting details about their crime on Facebook. It didn't take long for police to arrest them.

A robber in the United Kingdom got caught the old-fashioned way. After breaking into a house in Cambridge, he decided to take a nap. The owner came home, found him on the couch, and called the police. Case closed.

DO NOT CROSS
CRIME SCENE

Of course, most criminals are harder to find. In fact, many get away with their crimes for a while. It takes a mistake or good police work to put them in prison. And then there are some criminals who seem to pull off the perfect crimes. They leave the police baffled.

Maybe it's because the criminals are smart. Or maybe it's because they take huge risks. Or maybe it's both of those advantages mixed with some luck. These daring crimes can capture public imagination. They leave us asking, "How'd they do it?" or "Why'd they do it?" and "Could it happen again?"

CRIME SCENE
DO NOT CROSS

The "Dan Cooper" Hijacking

On November 24, 1971, a man went down in history for the most daring escape ever. Dan Cooper **hijacked** an airplane in Seattle, Washington, and received a huge **ransom**. After releasing all of the passengers, he demanded that the pilots fly the plane to Mexico.

But then Cooper did something shocking—he parachuted out of the plane. The conditions for skydiving were awful. It was cold and rainy. Cooper was jumping into the wooded mountains of the Pacific Northwest. Did he survive and disappear into the dense woods? Is his body still waiting to be found? Either way, Cooper's hijacking is one of the greatest unsolved crimes of all time.

hijack—to take illegal control of a vehicle, such as

Who Is Dan Cooper?

The hijacker only used the **alias** "Dan Cooper." But newspapers mistakenly reported his name as "D.B. Cooper," so most people remember Cooper by that name. Investigators know almost nothing about Cooper. But they do know that he boarded a plane in Portland, Oregon, that night. The flight to Seattle appeared to be routine. During the flight nobody really noticed Cooper.

Then Cooper took over the Boeing 727. He said he had a bomb and that he'd kill all of the passengers and crew if they didn't do what he asked. He demanded four parachutes and $200,000 in $20 bills. That amount is worth about $2.5 million today.

alias—a false name, especially one used by a criminal

The Jump

The plane landed in Seattle. Cooper released the passengers but not the pilots. As demanded, the Federal Bureau of Investigation (FBI) gave Cooper the parachutes and money. Cooper then ordered the plane to fly to Mexico. Shortly after, Cooper made his famous jump into the night. Even though police were following in other airplanes, they didn't see Cooper jump or where he landed.

Did Cooper Survive?

Few people believe Cooper survived the jump out of the plane. It's unlikely that he landed safely in such a heavily wooded area. Even if he did, his light clothing would not have protected him from the freezing temperatures for long. If Cooper is still alive today, he would have succeeded in one of the most daring crimes of all time.

One Solid Clue

The huge manhunt that followed Cooper's hijacking turned up almost nothing. The case grew very cold until 1980. That's when a boy playing near the Columbia River in Oregon found $5,800 in $20 bills. The **serial numbers** on the bills matched the money that Cooper had with him. A search of the area also uncovered a skull. But it was the skull of a woman.

FBI agents dig in a sandy beach on the Columbia River shoreline in Oregon. A portion of the Dan Cooper hijack money was found along the riverbank in 1980.

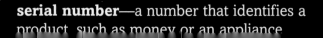

serial number—a number that identifies a product, such as money or an appliance

The Northern Bank Robbery

Right before Christmas in 2004, gang members in Belfast, Northern Ireland, pulled off a daring **heist**. On December 19, armed men posed as police officers to gain entry into two homes. One belonged to Chris Ward. The other belonged to Kevin McMullan. Both were executives at Northern Bank.

Robbers held the two families at gunpoint. Ward was taken to McMullan's house. Meanwhile McMullan's wife was taken to a forest south of Belfast. All of the family members remained **hostages**. Ward and McMullan were told to go into work the following day and act normal. If they tipped off anyone, their families would be killed.

Both men cooperated. At the end of the day, the two men led the robbers into the bank's underground **vault**. Both men had been selected because they had keys to the vault, and two keys were needed to get in. The robbers hauled away about $50 million in cash. It was the biggest all-cash robbery in the history of the United Kingdom.

heist—an armed robbery

hostage—a person held against his or her will

vault—a room or compartment for keeping money and other valuables safe

Leaving Few Clues Behind

The men involved knew exactly what to do to leave behind as little evidence as possible, including shaving off facial hair. They did this to avoid leaving behind anything that could provide DNA evidence to police, such as hair. DNA is a type of molecule that makes up each person's body. Most DNA molecules are unique. DNA evidence can be matched up to a certain person and prove that he or she committed a crime.

Newspaper headlines alerted the public about the Northern Bank heist shortly after the crime.

The Hostages

None of the hostages were killed. But they all suffered during the heist. McMullan's wife Karyn suffered the most. She had no warm clothing or shoes. She was also blindfolded for nearly 24 hours. But she managed to escape and alert police.

Who Pulled It Off?

Suspicion immediately fell on the Provisional Irish Republican Army (Provisional IRA). The Provisional IRA was a violent resistance group that wanted Northern Ireland to break away from the United Kingdom and join Ireland. The organization had a long history of pulling off violent robberies and kidnappings to fund its operations. The Northern Bank robbery was carried out so professionally that almost everyone assumed that the Provisional IRA was involved.

A Threat to Peace

The Northern Bank robbery was one of several crimes blamed on the Provisional IRA. Some members of the IRA have also been accused of murders and spying. Shortly before the robbery, however, the IRA announced it would end its armed campaign.

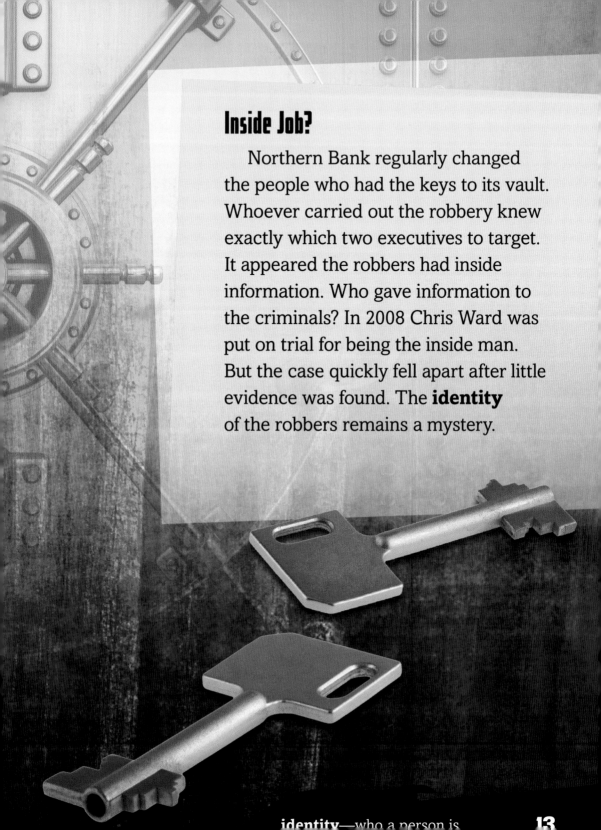

Inside Job?

Northern Bank regularly changed the people who had the keys to its vault. Whoever carried out the robbery knew exactly which two executives to target. It appeared the robbers had inside information. Who gave information to the criminals? In 2008 Chris Ward was put on trial for being the inside man. But the case quickly fell apart after little evidence was found. The **identity** of the robbers remains a mystery.

identity—who a person is

The Isabella Stewart Gardner
Museum Heist

In the early morning hours of March 18, 1990, robbers disguised as police officers entered Boston's Isabella Stewart Gardner Museum. Their disguises fooled the two night watchmen, who were quickly tied up. The thieves then made off with millions of dollars in valuable objects from the museum.

The stolen objects weren't just any works of art. They were 13 paintings and other objects made by world-famous masters like Rembrandt and Vermeer. Then the robbers and the art disappeared. However, the works of art were so well known that they couldn't simply be sold to any buyer. The robbers must have known someone who would buy the art in advance. Or maybe they wanted to keep the works themselves. Either way the thieves have **eluded** capture for more than 25 years.

elude—to escape or get away from someone

To Catch a Thief

In 2013 FBI agents said they knew the identity of the thieves. The FBI said the thieves were tied to a criminal organization based in the northeastern United States. Even if caught, however, the criminals could no longer be arrested for the thefts. The **statute** of limitations had run out. They could be arrested for possessing stolen property. But authorities say they will not press charges if the artwork is returned voluntarily.

Are They OK?

Officials at the Gardner Museum publicly urge the thieves to take care of the works. Old paintings can be especially **fragile** if not kept under the right conditions. Officials also worry that those who have the stolen art could destroy it on purpose to protect themselves from criminal charges.

The artwork stolen from the Gardner Museum is believed to be worth about $300 million. But such famous works of art could not be replaced. So in reality the stolen works are priceless.

The Gardner Museum has not replaced the works of art on its gallery walls. Instead it has left gaps where the works once were.

statute—a rule or a law
fragile—delicate or easily broken

The Lloyds Bank Robbery

In 1971 a group of thieves set out to break into Lloyds Bank in London. Their goal was to get to the bank's most secure room. The secure room contained safe deposit boxes. Safe deposit boxes are where people store their most valuable possessions for safety. Oftentimes these boxes hold diamonds, jewelry, and large amounts of cash.

EXIT TO BANK
9 BY 15 INCHES

LENGTH 40 FEET

BANK BASEMENT
SOLID CONCRETE

10524

10574

10525

10526

10527

The thieves' plan for getting into the room was clever and dangerous. They were going to tunnel under the bank and break in through the floor. In order to do that, they had to rent out a store two doors away, close it down, and start the tunnel there. On top of that, they had to tunnel under a restaurant in-between. They could only dig on weekends when all the shops were closed to avoid making noise when people were around.

The work took months. But when the crooks finally did get in, they made off with **loot** worth nearly $60 million in today's money. It was one of the boldest bank robberies ever.

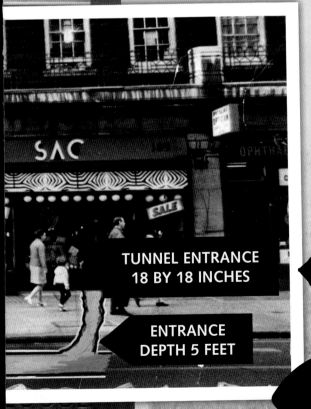

SAC

TUNNEL ENTRANCE 18 BY 18 INCHES

ENTRANCE DEPTH 5 FEET

The rented shop was close to the bank, allowing the crooks to gain underground entrance.

loot—stolen money or valuables

19

Walkie-Talkie Chatter

The robbers put a lookout on a roof and communicated with **walkie-talkies** during the robbery. A nearby radio operator overheard their talk and realized what was happening. He called the police. The police should have been able to figure out which bank was being robbed. But they decided to search too large of an area, and the robbers got away.

Who Committed the Crime?

Police found four men connected to the crime because of a foolish mistake. One of the men signed his real name when he rented the store where the tunnel started. Police immediately looked for known criminal **associates**. The rest of the thieves were soon arrested and imprisoned for the robbery.

But their arrest raised many questions. All of them had been small-time thieves. None of them had ever shown the skills needed to dig tunnels. None had ever used heavy equipment or explosives. All of those skills were needed for the Lloyds Bank burglary. Because of that, many police believed others were involved or another criminal **mastermind** was behind it. But nobody else has ever been caught.

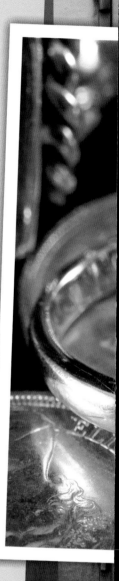

10524

Safe deposit boxes at Lloyds Bank held people's important valuables, such as money and jewelry. None of the loot from the robbery has ever been found or returned to its rightful owners.

10531

10532

walkie-talkie—a radio that is held in the hand, powered by batteries, and is used to communicate over short distances

associate—a companion or comrade

mastermind—a person who plans and controls the way an action is carried out

Tylenol Poisonings

On September 29, 1982, 12-year-old Mary Kellerman's parents gave her Extra-Strength Tylenol to help her feel better. But the capsules held a deadly ingredient. Someone had added small amounts of a poison called cyanide to the bottle. Within the next few days, six others were poisoned the same way. Four of them, including Mary, died. All of them lived near Chicago, Illinois.

People around the world panicked. Nobody felt safe consuming bottled medicines. Millions threw away their Tylenol and other pills. Tylenol was pulled from store shelves.

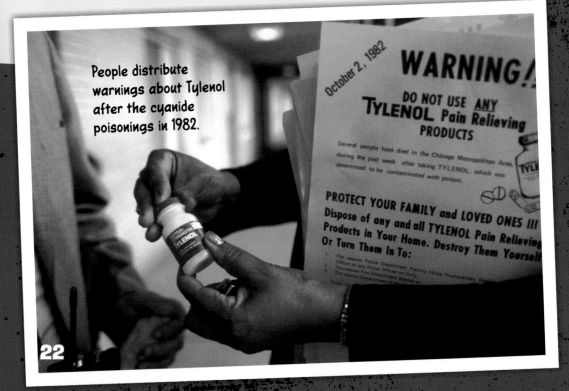

People distribute warnings about Tylenol after the cyanide poisonings in 1982.

October 2, 1982

WARNING!

DO NOT USE ANY TYLENOL Pain Relieving PRODUCTS

Several people have died in the Chicago Metropolitan Area during the past week after taking TYLENOL, which was determined to be contaminated with poison.

PROTECT YOUR FAMILY and LOVED ONES !!! Dispose of any and all TYLENOL Pain Relieving Products in Your Home. Destroy Them Yourself Or Turn Them In To:

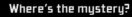

Ongoing Investigation

Police cars in the Chicago area cruised up and down streets, warning people over loudspeakers not to use Tylenol. Despite a huge police search, no killer was ever found.

One man wrote a ransom note demanding money to stop the poisonings. He was caught, but police soon discovered that he could not have committed the murders. Others were investigated. But no clear answer has ever been found. Nobody knows why the poisonings took place.

Big Changes

In the United States, bottled pills like Tylenol were packaged differently after the 1982 incident. Food and drug makers came up with **tamper**-proof packages with seals. The new packaging made it much more difficult for someone to add poison or other dangerous substances to pill bottles.

tamper—to interfere with something so that it becomes damaged or broken

The Springfield Three

On June 7, 1992, Stacy McCall, Suzanne "Suzie" Streeter, and Suzie's mother, Sherrill Levitt, vanished from Levitt's home in Springfield, Missouri. The three women haven't been seen since.

Friends and neighbors did not realize that they had disappeared until the next day. Stacy, 18, and Suzie, 19, were supposed to meet up with friends. They had just graduated from high school and were supposed to go to several parties. Friends came looking for them when they didn't show up. All of the women's personal property—including purses, cars, and keys—were left behind. Stacy's mom called the police.

Where Are They?

The three disappearances remain a mystery. There have been several **suspects**. The lead suspect for a short time was Robert Craig Cox. He is a convicted kidnapper who is also suspected of murder. Cox, who is in prison for another crime, has hinted that he knows what happened to the women. But police fear Cox lied to get attention. Police assume that the three women were murdered. But no bodies have ever been found.

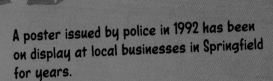

A poster issued by police in 1992 has been on display at local businesses in Springfield for years.

MISSING

Sherrill Levitt
Age 47

Suzie Streeter
Age 19

Stacy McCall
Age 18

Call Springfield, Missouri Police Department
(417) 864-1700

suspect—someone who may
be responsible for a crime

Amsterdam Diamond Heist

On February 25, 2005, a daring diamond heist took place at Schiphol Airport in Amsterdam, Netherlands. Two men dressed as workers for the Dutch airline KLM arrived at the cargo terminal. But they weren't workers. They arrived in a stolen KLM car. The men then stopped a truck near a runway. It was driving up to a KLM airplane. The truck was carrying millions of dollars worth of diamonds.

The robbery was clever because it was so simple. The truck carrying the diamonds had two drivers. The armed robbers stopped the truck and forced the two drivers to lie facedown on the ground. Many people were watching as this happened. But the robbery went so quickly that no one could stop it. The robbers got in the truck and casually drove off with the diamonds.

The final price tag for this infamous European heist was around $118 million. That makes it the world's biggest diamond robbery.

Schiphol Amsterdam

Security

The security at Schiphol Airport was surprisingly relaxed. Two weeks before the robbery, four men stole a KLM cargo truck and uniforms. This burglary allowed the men to move around in secure areas of the airport and even practice their robbery. No one realized this was happening until after the crime.

Any Suspects?

The robbers have not been seen since. Their truck was later found, but the robbers and the diamonds were gone. The type of diamonds stolen made it harder to track them. Many of the diamonds were **uncut**. These types of diamonds are much harder to track than cut diamonds because there are fewer records of them. The thieves could easily pass them off as newly discovered diamonds to diamond buyers.

uncut diamonds

uncut—not shaped by cutting, especially precious stones or diamonds

History's Unsolved Crimes

Nothing stirs the imagination quite like unsolved crimes. Huge sums of money, stolen works of art, and mysterious disappearances capture people's interest. Police and authorities work hard to crack these cases. Is Dan Cooper still alive somewhere? Was the Provisional IRA involved in the 2004 Northern Bank robbery in Belfast? Where are the diamonds that were stolen in Amsterdam in 2005? Such questions might never be answered.

Glossary

alias (AY-lee-uhss)—a false name, especially one used by a criminal

associate (uh-SOH-see-eyt)—a companion or comrade

elude (i-LUDE)—to escape or get away from someone

fragile (FRAJ-il)—delicate or easily broken

heist (HEIST)—an armed robbery

hijack (HYE-jak)—to take illegal control of a vehicle, such as an airplane

hostage (HOSS-tij)—a person held against his or her will

identity (eye-DEN-ti-tee)—who a person is

loot (LOOT)—stolen money or valuables

mastermind (MASS-tur-minde)—a person who plans and controls the way an action is carried out

ransom (RAN-suhm)—money or objects that are demanded before someone who is being held captive can be set free

serial number (SIHR-ee-uhl NUHM-ber)—a number that identifies a product, such as money or an appliance

statute (STACH-oot)—a rule or a law

suspect (SUHSS-pekt)—someone who may be responsible for a crime

tamper (TAM-pur)—to interfere with something so that it becomes damaged or broken

uncut (uhn-KUHT)—not shaped by cutting, especially precious stones or diamonds

vault (VAWLT)—a room or compartment for keeping money and other valuables safe

walkie-talkie (WAW-kee TAW-kee)—a radio that is held in the hand, powered by batteries, and is used to communicate over short distances

Read More

Guillain, Charlotte. *Great Art Thefts.* Treasure Hunters. Chicago: Capstone Raintree, 2013.

Orr, Tamra B. *Investigating a Crime Scene.* Science Explorer: Follow the Clues. Ann Arbor, Mich.: Cherry Lake Publishing, 2014.

Peppas, Lynn. *Forensics: The Scene of the Crime.* Crabtree Chrome. New York: Crabtree Pub., 2015.

Internet Sites

FactHound offers a safe, fun way to find Internet sites related to this book. All of the sites on FactHound have been researched by our staff.

Here's all you do:

Visit *www.facthound.com*

Type in this code: 9781491442630

Check out projects, games and lots more at
www.capstonekids.com

Index